CAFÉ FLORES

ESCAPE TO ITALY

HOLLY GREENE

CONTENTS

CHAPTER 1

SARAH PARKER CROSSED AND RECROSSED HER legs as she sat in Rome's Da Vinci airport terminal, trying to concentrate on the paperback novel in her hands.

It was the latest from Lily Forbes – one of her favourite UK novelists – called *No Ocean Too Wide,* but for all she tried, Sarah couldn't focus on the words on the page.

Overhead there was an announcement in Italian which she didn't understand; she supposed that before jetting off to Italy she should have studied a bit of the language, but she hadn't found the time.

She twisted her head, scanning the lounge for any sign of her husband, with no luck.

Nate had gone to argue with the airline

about their lost luggage and insisted that she find a cosy place to tuck herself up with a book and some coffee while she waited.

"It might take a while," he'd said before disappearing into the terminal, and while she normally would have taken his words as a chivalrous indication that he didn't want her to tax herself with waiting, right now she wasn't so sure.

She almost imagined her new husband leaning against an airport counter with relief, glad to be away from her for a few moments.

She couldn't say she'd blame him, or that she didn't feel the same way.

For a honeymoon, this trip was turning out to be anything but romantic.

Italy wasn't even their original destination; nor for that matter was it strictly a honeymoon, coming two months after their wedding.

In fact, as Sarah's mind drifted back over the past few months, she thought that it was a wonder this trip had happened at all.

Truthfully, she couldn't say the trouble had started with the wedding. If anything, it had started when she first brought Nate home to meet her parents in Chicago two years prior.

They had met through friends during their last year of college and had been instantly smitten.

Her parents were not so enthusiastic.

Over dinner, they had drilled Nate subtly but relentlessly about all things related to his schooling, job prospects and family ties, and in the end, he was weighed and found wanting.

Sarah's parents raised an eyebrow when they learned Nate's father was a self-made man (a term her dad used with prim derision) and that he didn't come from *old money* (as her father did).

Later Sarah overheard her mother whispering on the telephone with a friend.

"And can you just believe," she'd said, in a horrified tone usually associated with natural disasters or some type of scandal in the family, "I think his mother actually works for a living?"

Her parents' disapproval notwithstanding, Sarah was smitten with Nate and vice versa, and as things progressed naturally between the two an engagement was soon announced.

That, Sarah decided, was when things began to go sideways at an alarming rate.

Of course she had met Nate's parents and she thought she got on with them pretty well.

His family was different to hers, but overall she thought she'd made a good impression (despite a moment of awkwardness when she complimented their cook on the dessert and learned that they had no such domestic help). Nate later told her that his parents found her 'charming' and Sarah revelled in the bliss that comes with being young and in love.

Then it was time to announce their engagement, and for their parents to meet. The tension between the two families was palpable from the start.

It was clear that the Fieldings were going through with this show of unity and affection only to please their daughter, but that they were not prepared to be anything less than frosty to the Parker family that so clearly belonged to another social class.

For their part, Nate's parents were to all appearances perfectly civil, but Sarah could sense resentment underneath their outward politeness.

She and Nate shared an optimistic view that perhaps over time their respective sets of parents would thaw out enough to share in the joy of the upcoming wedding; but if anything, the launch of wedding preparations turned the early tension into all-out hostility.

Sarah's parents wanted a spring wedding; the Parkers felt this would be a crowded time and wanted to know why the young couple didn't go with something less showy and traditional.

The families began a drawn-out tug-of-war over everything from venues to wedding colours to the guest list; the final straw came when Sarah's mother announced firmly that no children under the age of ten would be allowed in the wedding pictures unless they proved themselves to be perfectly behaved for the camera, since, after all, 'nothing ruins a wedding picture more quickly than an ugly, crying child.'

Little by little, Sarah watched the wedding of her dreams slip away through her fingers. Her voice could barely be heard over the demands of her parents and future in-laws, both of whom seemed determined to steer the wedding as much to their tastes as possible.

Nate seemed cool about the whole thing though.

"Why don't we just elope, if it's all so stress-ful?" he asked one night, while the young couple tried to enjoy a quiet dinner out to get away from all the wedding drama.

In retrospect Sarah supposed he meant the offer in kindness, and as an out from the burden of all the planning, but at the time she took it as a complaint and lashed out, berating him for not understanding what a fairy-tale wedding would mean to her.

The night ended poorly, as so many of their nights together seemed to since he'd first got down on one knee.

In the end, miraculously, Nate and Sarah married on a warm April day in front of nearly four hundred guests; the ceremony took place outdoors at the private estate of a friend of her father's.

She wore a custom-made strapless silk Vera Wang gown and hand-dyed Christian Louboutin heels and a pearl seed-studded veil that had arrived packed in layer upon layer of tissue paper.

There were thousands of dollars worth of lilies at the ceremony—her mother's favourite flower—and she was surprised and delighted when a flock of doves was set loose immediately following their vows, fluttering gently over the guests to the "oohs and "aahs"s of the crowd.

For a short moment, she thought that all of the stress of the past months was behind them, and they were ready for the bliss of married life.

Boy, had she been wrong….

CHAPTER 2

Lily Forbes strode purposefully through the airport, heels clicking on the floor, sunglasses firmly in place, carry-on suitcase rolling along neatly behind her.

She didn't expect to be recognized by anyone—this was something actresses and pop singers had to worry about, not writers—but all the same, she considered this trip to be equal parts business and pleasure (with a heavy emphasis on pleasure) and she didn't want to be bothered if she could avoid it.

It was with relief that she hailed a taxi outside the terminal and dropped into the backseat to rest her tired feet.

She supposed she should have been practical and worn flats for her trip, but when you're approaching forty you can't be caught slacking, she thought, as she wiggled her toes out of one sleek calf-hair Manolo and stretched her foot gratefully.

Not that she had anything to worry about, really—though in her mid-forties she was as trim now as she had been in her twenties, and judicious tanning and trips to the salon had kept her skin smooth and glowing and any stray greys in her hair at bay.

Still, there was no sense in being careless, especially in stylish Italy.

She thought ruefully of some of her less-cautious thirty-something friends who had begun to adopt a uniform of yoga pants and velour zip-up hoodies as they ferried their children to after-school activities.

Some of them no longer even bothered to wear mascara, for goodness sake. But not Lily.

She leaned back in her seat and looked approvingly out the window, noting the late afternoon sun and the architecture of the city of Verona, just visible from a distance. She certainly wouldn't be accused of neglecting herself.

A successful and high-profile career as a novelist certainly helped though; she had plenty of money to splash out on facials and a personal trainer.

She also had a tastefully decorated London apartment and a wardrobe to inspire envy in any fashion editor. An international bestselling author, Lily had everything she could want, and the ability to jet away to Italy in the name of 'research' was just one of the perks.

There was only one small thing she lacked: a love life.

She almost laughed out loud as the taxi pulled away from the gleaming airport terminal and into traffic.

Wouldn't her loyal fans just gasp to hear that?

Lily Forbes, unlucky in love. Because it was true: under all the layers of success and the luxurious lifestyle she'd cultivated, there was a gaping hole in Lily's life that should have been filled by a relationship.

While all her friends went on to marry and settle down with children, she seemed to be caught in an endless string of dead-end relationships.

Not that a white dress, a house in the suburbs and 2.5 children were what she desired; she wasn't the type to bleat pitifully that she could only be fulfilled as a wife and mother.

She loved her career, loved the independence and enjoyed life's luxuries. But whenever she saw a couple smiling at each other in a café, or walking hand in hand down the street, she felt a small twinge in her chest.

Why couldn't romance be as simple for her as it was for the characters in her books?

She thought of some of the recent fan mail she received. *Dear Miss Forbes*, read a typical letter or e-mail: *Where can I meet the heroes in your novels? I've never read anything so romantic. I can't put them down until the last page.*

Her last novel *No Ocean Too Wide*, had enjoyed a good run on the Sunday Times best-seller list; the mass-market paperbacks were out now and she'd seen some in the stands in the airport lounge at Heathrow.

The success of that book however, had been both a blessing and a curse.

She'd booked this Italian trip after a long and decidedly unpleasant chat with her agent, who reminded her that the follow-up manuscript was past the deadline.

The truth was that Lily hadn't yet even begun writing it, and she'd begged, pleaded and stormed for a delivery extension, but in the end, there was no way around it: *No Ocean Too Wide* had left readers panting for more, and her publisher wanted the next script by the end of the year.

Unfortunately Lily just wasn't in a good place to write about romance now. She'd finished the previous book just as she was embarking on a promising string of dates with a city trader who lived in Dorset but worked in Central London.

She always wrote her best work when she was in love, or the mood for love, and their hot and heavy relationship had provided ample fuel for some of the novel's best bodice-ripping scenes.

Unfortunately for her, a few months of whirlwind romance ground to a halt when he abruptly dumped her.

Lily suspected his wandering eye meant he'd been doing more in London than mere business, and while she hadn't been particularly thinking about a long-term relationship in any case, the whole thing had soured her mood.

It was merely the latest in a long string of failed romances and with each successive one, she felt herself becoming more jaded and bitter about love.

Maybe at one time she'd believed in things like love at first sight, or true love uniting two people against all odds, and that breathless optimism has certainly made for a few great novels at the start of her career.

But now Lily felt burned out.

A heart broken too many times over had led her to believe that romance was just a ploy used to sell diamonds, flowers (and books), and that true love was not an option for most people.

Maybe a few women *thought* they had found it, but really they just hadn't discovered the warts on their frog princes yet. Soon enough something would happen to break the spell and like Lily, they would realise that true love was nothing more than a fairytale.

But with her agent breathing down her neck and her publisher's deadline looming, Lily knew that drastic measures were called for.

Hence this trip to Italy; first Rome for a spot of shopping, and then onwards to the city of Verona.

Where better to find inspiration for a romantic novel than the setting of one of the greatest love stories of all time, Romeo and Juliet?

Secretly Lily suspected that Verona would be brimming with starry-eyed tourists dreaming of their own Romeos, and her inner cynic was prepared to spend a lot of time elbowing her way through crowds.

She certainly didn't expect to feel much of a romantic vibe there, but she thought she might at least find some nice locations and authentic on-the-ground local flavour.

And if nothing else, it would be a nice sunshine break filled with food, wine and shopping, before she returned to London to work on the book in earnest.

The traffic flowed on around her as the car travelled on — she glanced with some interest at the views of the countryside sliding by, but her mind was elsewhere.

She kept trying to come up with something to use as a good start for the book.

Jilted bride travels to Verona and meets the man of her dreams? No, that was too similar to the plot of *Honeymoon for One.* (Although, to be fair, in that novel, her heroine at least went through with the wedding—it was after the ceremony that she caught her husband with one of her bridesmaids...)

She drummed her fingers on the car seat.

Perhaps her heroine could be newly divorced and spending some of the cash from the settlement on a European holiday... But she'd done something similar with *Around the World For Love*, sending her divorcee on a worldwide hunt for romance.

What about a heroine who keeps bumping into the same unlikeable male traveller and comes to realise he's actually her soulmate? (Done to death in general though she decided glumly, and very similar to her characters-on-a-delayed-flight scenario of *Stopover to Love*).

Try as she might, Lily couldn't bring her travel-wearied brain to come up with a decent plot along those lines.

Hell, what if there just wasn't anything original left for her to write?

At last, she arrived at her hotel and momentarily set aside the problem of her book.

She'd requested one of the best suites—no expense spared—and Lily already had plans to order in this evening rather than go out for dinner, complete with a bottle of excellent Italian wine.

It was only Thursday after all, and she had plenty of time over the weekend to explore Verona and gather inspiration for her novel.

For now, she intended to have a long bubble bath, a quiet dinner and an early bedtime.

Tomorrow she'd set out on her quest to trace the story of Romeo and Juliet, and perhaps come up with a few choice locations for her story.

For now, Lily needed her beauty sleep.

CHAPTER 3

Declan O'Neill collected his luggage from the baggage carousel and hailed a taxi outside the terminal with minimal interaction with his fellow passengers or the Aer Lingus crew.

His flight from Dublin had not been uncomfortable and he wasn't particularly tired, at least not in a physical sense.

All the same, as he slumped into the car and gave mumbled directions to the driver, he felt a powerful sense of exhaustion.

He wanted only to find his hotel and crawl into bed for the evening. Even so, on the short drive into the centre of Verona, he found that his mind was restless.

The fatigue that had plagued him on the

flight earlier had been replaced by a nervous energy, denying him the one thing he desired most: sleep.

At least if he could sleep, he could see her.

He stared out the window of the car, not really seeing anything past his reflection in the glass.

Absentmindedly he twisted the thin gold band on his finger. He'd passed the year in something of a fog, trying to remember her while selectively forgetting so many things: the painful gauntness of her cheeks during her last months, the way she'd tried so hard not to show that she was in pain, the way she mostly slept through her days and nights at the end.

The reason she'd insisted that he take this very trip.

It had been almost one year since his beloved wife's death.

It was a fairly mild day at the start of June, sunny and calm. Hannah had been having one of her better days, and he'd carried her out onto their backyard and fixed her up with blankets and a cool drink in her favourite wicker chair.

The disease ravaging her body and merciless rounds of chemo treatment had left her frail, and even with the warm summer temperatures she pulled the covers tighter around her body.

Declan sat next to her, mute with the pain of holding back the lump in his throat, trying not to grip her hand too tightly for fear of hurting her.

It was Hannah who broke the silence first. "Love, I want you to do me a favour."

He sat up straighter, instantly alert. "Anything," he said, hoping his voice wouldn't crack.

"It's a big favour," she said tiredly, trying to smile and he tried to smile back.

"There's nothing I wouldn't do for you. Tell me and I'll do it."

"I want you to do something after...after I'm gone." Declan gripped her hand a little more tightly despite himself, but he forced himself to keep quiet. "I want you to make a trip next year. To Italy. Will you do that?"

Declan opened his mouth to ask why, but the look on his wife's face was so pleading, so hopeful, that instead, he could only say, "Of course."

And so it all was settled.

Hannah wanted him to make a trip to the city of Verona on the anniversary of her death.

He'd protested, struck by the horrible unfairness of it all.

When they had married as young twenty-somethings, they'd had little enough money to start their married life let alone for a honeymoon.

Hannah, ever the romantic, had dreamed of a trip to Italy, and especially of a weekend in Verona; she researched the city online and was constantly telling him little tidbits about its history, particularly as the romantic backdrop to the tragic love story of Romeo and Juliet.

Declan never quite shared her fascination, but nonetheless, he would have loved nothing more than to spirit her away for a weekend there, if only money permitted.

But life doesn't always give us what we want, and money and schedules never quite allowed the holiday they'd envisioned.

And as the years rolled by Declan and Hannah found plenty of happiness in their life together that the dream of travelling to Italy slowly died away, a nice thought that had just never come to fruition.

There were no children, which he knew saddened Hannah, especially as their tenth anniversary came and went; but as they moved into their mid-thirties they were both still head over heels in love, and having just moved out of a small Dublin apartment and into a new home in the suburbs, they were perfectly busy and content with painting, gardening, and everything else that goes with creating a little bubble of domestic bliss together.

Then came the long bouts of fatigue, the dizzy spells, the doctor visits, the diagnosis.

Almost before Declan and Hannah could adjust to the shock, their lives had been taken over by the cancer and then by the treatments, which after a while nearly seemed worse than the illness itself.

Declan clung desperately to hope even as he sat up in the dead of night, watching his wife breathe and wondering if this night would be her last.

When the time finally came only eight months after that first visit to the specialist, Declan was so numb with grief that he moved through his days as if on autopilot.

There were so many things to do and to wrap up in the wake of her death, and in a way, it was a blessing in disguise that he had no time to stop and think.

But as the days turned into weeks and then

into months, he kept coming back to the letter she'd written for him in her last days and secretly tucked away for him to read, reminding him of his promise and urging him to go on the trip they'd never taken together.

People tell me the first year is the hardest, she'd written, and the smudges in the ink showed she must have been tired, dragging her hand across the page. *I don't want you to be alone on that day. I know you never fell in love with the idea of Verona like I did, but I think once you're there you'll feel me with you, at least in spirit. And I hope that something there will help you feel whole again.*

Declan had the letter with him; carefully folded and tucked away in his suitcase. He liked to smooth out the creases and look at the familiar handwriting; if he closed his eyes he could almost smell her perfume.

He still didn't understand it, but a promise was a promise, and he would do anything to honour Hannah's memory.

As tired and unhappy as he felt, he had dutifully purchased a guidebook to the city of Verona and mapped out a series of tours and activities for his weekend, all based on places he thought she might have enjoyed.

The Casa di Giulietta as it was called was

supposedly the family home of the famous Juliet from Shakespeare's story and a popular tourist destination in the city.

People flocked to her balcony and a wall where lovelorn young women (and maybe men too? he wondered idly) pinned up letters to Juliet, hoping for assistance in all matters of the heart.

Declan figured he could do with some of that himself; namely, ask Juliet if he'd even be able to get over his own heartbreak.

CHAPTER 4

"IT'S NO GOOD," NATE SAID WEARILY, SITTING down next to his new wife. "The airline says our luggage was mistakenly rerouted on another flight. We won't get it for another couple of days, at least. I've left them the name of our hotel in Verona."

Sarah's heart sank. Why did everything seem to be going wrong all the time?

"Well, I guess that's that, then."

"Yeah. A good thing we packed carry-on bags after all."

Sarah bit her tongue at this remark. They'd had a last-minute argument while packing for the trip when she announced that she planned to skip the carry-on; after all, she was only taking one suitcase, so why the extra hassle of an additional bag?

Nate, a more seasoned traveller, patiently explained that in the event something happened to their bags, she would be glad to have a change of clothes and her toothbrush at hand.

She'd told him he was worrying needlessly, and he'd implied that she never worried enough.

Sarah thought that now he just couldn't resist the chance to rub in the fact that he'd been proved right after all.

She closed her book and stood, pretending to ignore his remark. This was supposed to be a honeymoon, after all; she didn't want to start their stay in Italy with an airport spat. Instead, she said only, "Shall we find a taxi?"

"Of course." He followed her lead. "What are you reading? Oh, just that. Should've known."

This time Sarah really was tempted to say something cutting, but she satisfied herself with shooting him a withering look instead.

He raised his eyebrows innocently and brushed past her to move through the terminal.

He'd never made a secret of his disdain for her choice of reading material and often teased her about the romantic 'nonsense' she liked to read.

"So what?" she would say. "I enjoy it and that's all that matters." Today, though, she wasn't in the mood to tease or to be teased, and she jammed the book into her bag and followed Nate sullenly to the taxi stand.

The couple had a bit of a wait for a taxi, but at last, they were inside and en route to the train station that would take them from Rome to Verona, where they had planned to spend a long, romantic weekend.

An uneasy silence reigned in the backseat of the car, with Nate and Sarah purposefully avoiding looking at each other or speaking in anything more than monosyllables.

Sarah wasn't sure if the Italian taxi driver didn't speak much English or if he could sense by their mood that this wasn't a time for small talk, but in any case, he drove without speaking to them, and she lapsed back into her own memories.

The wedding. Oh, it had indeed been beautiful.

But immediately afterwards, things started falling to pieces once more. Sarah had had her heart set on a honeymoon on a tropical Indonesian island since she'd been a teenager, and they'd originally made arrangements to fly to Bali for a two-week stay, complete with rooms in those cute little huts above the water and plenty of time to sun themselves on the beach during the day.

They arranged to fly into San Francisco and spend a night there before leaving the U.S. for their trip, but the next morning at their hotel they received a phone call from Nate's parents: his brother had been in a car accident leaving the wedding and was in serious condition at the hospital.

Sarah swallowed her disappointment and told Nate that of course, they had to cancel and return home; this was a family emergency, after all.

But the honeymoon was not easily rescheduled. His brother recovered slowly and Nate was determined to stay in Chicago to help him as long as he was needed.

Then there were troubles re-booking the hotel.

Sarah began to suspect that Nate didn't really care about going after all when he expressed a lack of interest in helping her reschedule the trip; that led to another argument.

The stress of their courtship, wedding and the weeks following it were beginning to wear on the newly married couple, and small disagreements were becoming a regular part of their life together now.

Sarah hoped desperately that a belated honeymoon would give them a fresh start and allow them to put this bumpy period behind them.

At last, they had come to an agreement.

An old school friend had holidayed in Italy the previous year and raved about the delights of Verona; the romantic atmosphere, the food, the art, and the feeling of stepping into another world where the stresses of everyday life did not exist.

It sounded perfect to Sarah, and she booked their stay immediately.

Of course, the plans for the trip itself did not go smoothly either.

There was the argument about the luggage; the unexpected fees to fast-track an up-to-date passport (which led to another casual remark from Nate to his new bride that she didn't plan things out far enough in advance).

They were also forced to adjust their travel plans at the last minute when incredibly a summer storm meant that their direct flight from Chicago to Verona was cancelled, forcing them to scramble for an alternative stop in Rome and endure a series of unpleasant (and time-consuming) layovers, delaying them still further from their elusive romantic honeymoon.

And now to top it all off, the misplaced luggage was to be forwarded to their hotel no sooner than Sunday. And it was now only Thursday afternoon!

Sarah gazed out the window of the taxi and tried to lose herself in the sights and sounds of the Italian capital, for what little time they'd be here.

The taxi reached the train station in short order, and they boarded in the same stiff silence that had reigned throughout their flight and taxi ride.

They'd been told that the train journey to Verona would take about three hours, and Sarah pulled out her novel once more - pointedly ignoring Nate's expression of irritation - determined to lose herself in it as they travelled.

However, after an hour or so, she put it back in her bag, gradually becoming absorbed by the view from the train window.

The countryside was bathed in soft sunshine as sunset approached, and the golden light only enhanced the beauty of the scene.

Sarah scooted closer to the window to gaze out at the gentle roll of hills, farms and lavender fields dusky in the last rays of light, trees casting gentle shadows over white-washed family homes and terracotta roofs.

It was a captivating scene, and she couldn't help but feel enchanted as she watched the countryside roll by.

She noticed that Nate had also moved closer to the window to look out as the scenery flew by them.

The train entered the outskirts of Verona at dusk, but even in the fading light Sarah caught a small glimpse of what the city had to offer.

The old stone architecture was impressive even in the falling gloom, and she craned her neck for a better look at the old buildings.

She'd expected a fusion of modern and classical in this city, but she hadn't been prepared for how much old-world charm the city exuded.

Once the couple were in another taxi en route to their hotel she kept her face to the window of the car, peering excitedly at the city streets.

Iron gates and winding cobbled paths whispered of another time, before the arrival of modern things like automobiles.

Balconies trailed with vines abloom with summer flowers, and Sarah could almost imagine their fragrance.

She felt as though she were truly slipping into another world.

It was a beautiful city and unmistakably romantic.

She couldn't read a single one of the many signs in Italian, but even the look of the language was charming and exquisite.

She caught sight of couples sitting outside of trattorias, enjoying their evening meals as day turned to night, and she felt a small pang of jealousy mixed with hope.

They all looked so carefree, sipping wine and savouring their food together.

Instantly Sarah felt her mood lighten and

decided that by the end of this stay, she and Nate would be among those happy couples, talking and laughing as though they hadn't a care in the world.

Whether he liked it or not.

CHAPTER 5

LILY PERMITTED HERSELF THE LUXURY OF sleeping in on her first morning in Verona—and why not? She was on holiday, after all.

When she finally woke she yawned and stretched like a cat, dropping her sleeping mask on the bedside table and slipping into a silk robe to go out onto the balcony.

Luckily her room had a little coffeemaker sitting on the bureau, so she was able to brew a cup of espresso to enjoy while she woke up.

The view from the balcony wasn't bad.

Much of Verona, for having been modernised over the past few decades, still retained a distinctly rustic charm, and architecture that made it look like it had one foot still firmly planted in another era.

There was some sound of traffic from the main streets (several blocks away from her hotel, thankfully—she couldn't sleep with the sound of heavy traffic) but here it was mostly peaceful, and in the distance, she could see the sun shining on the Adige River.

It was a pleasant morning, seasonally warm and inviting, and the perfect day for a little sightseeing.

Lily dressed for the day in slim-cut jeans, stylish flats and a cashmere scarf just in case the weather turned chilly.

She went down to the dining room and dithered a bit over breakfast, finally settling on fruit and yoghurt with just a small pastry on the side—a little concession, and one that she was sure she could walk off during her sight-seeing that day.

Outside the air was warming up and promising a beautiful day for sight-seeing, and Lily decided to take a taxi across town to visit one of the main attractions in Verona, the Casa di Giulietta.

She was sure the place would be packed with tourists vying for a chance to stand on the balcony and reenact scenes from *Romeo and*

Juliet with lovers and friends, but she wanted to take at least a peek at the house.

She honestly didn't have that much interest in the rest of the historical attractions of the city, at least for the moment.

It wasn't that she disliked history, art or architecture and on another trip, she might have found a bit of general sight-seeing to be amusing, but she grudgingly admitted that at this point she needed to focus on her work first and fun second.

If she visited the romantic historical site and didn't feel an immediate surge of inspiration, she might permit herself a bit of wandering through piazzas and museums for the rest of the day.

The taxi didn't take long to zip across the city and deposit her in front of the old structure, and she stepped out to survey her surroundings.

Unlike many of the women visiting the site, Lily didn't place a high romantic value on the house, or the story of Romeo and Juliet themselves, for that matter.

She thought it most likely that the house had nothing whatsoever to do with star-crossed lovers, or that Juliet's famous balcony had never been used for poetic declarations of love or secret assignations in the face of disapproving rival families.

It was just another house, one that some enterprising soul had thought to fix up and market as the home of one of the most famous romantic heroines in history.

Lily couldn't exactly say that she disapproved either.

After all, someone had clearly made a smart move that had paid off beyond their wildest dreams; the courtyard of the old stone building was packed with camera-toting tourists.

And in truth, it *was* a romantic place to imagine a doomed heroine; the old brick masonry of the building was interrupted by small Gothic windows and large arched doorways leading to shady interiors, and there was an abundance of greenery still trailing down some of the walls.

Iron sconces, now fitted with electrical wiring, could have once held lanterns casting dim candlelight over the cobblestones at night.

Lily had brought a small notebook in her shoulder bag to jot down any scenes or thoughts that came to mind, and she quickly recorded these thoughts on the house as they struck her.

'Juliet's balcony' itself was fairly simple, made of stone and actually much smaller than she'd imagined.

Inside the house itself was cool but not dark, thanks to discreetly installed modern lights. The Casa had some old-world tiling on the floor and an elaborately panelled ceiling.

The theme of stone arches continued inside, with arches and pillars separating the rooms of the house, and from here Lily had a better look at the iron lattice of the windows and door panels.

There was a bit of furniture and art scattered throughout the rooms, and she took a while to examine all of the informational placards on the walls.

According to the information the house dated back to the 1200s and had sustained heavy damage over the years, leading to judicious restorations with architectural elements of the Medieval Age to help preserve the look and feel of the home as it would have been when Juliet was alive.

(*If* thought Lily, but kept that thought to herself.)

She had to admit that a lot of care had gone into refurbishing the old house, and the collection of costumes inside gave an interesting peek at life in old Verona.

Lily scribbled more notes as she went and snapped a few more pictures for reference.

As much as she was impressed with the historical details of the house, she couldn't shake off her inner cynic as she watched the crowds.

Giddy young women were going up to the balcony to declare dramatically, "What light through yonder window breaks?" or the closest thing they could manage before dissolving into fits of laughter while their friends snapped pictures from below or called for moody Instagram poses leaning on the balcony railing.

Tourists were murmuring excitedly over the costumes and historical placards throughout the house, as though a real celebrity had once graced these rooms.

For her part, Lily thought that it was a whole lot of nonsense. In all likelihood, Juliet Capulet had never existed, or if she had, her story was certainly not as dramatic as Shakespeare had made it out to be.

According to her sparse research, the Bard

wasn't even the first writer to dramatise this sort of story, which made her suspect he wrote it more to capitalise on a public thirst for drama than out of any sudden stirring of inspiration over two dead young lovers.

And who thought that the story was romantic, anyway? Lily didn't understand the pull. Oh, sure, the whole star-crossed lovers part was nice, but the suicide in a crypt? Not so much.

She preferred love stories where the hero and heroine escaped alive and intact, and could continue their romance happily ever after.

Mentally she composed her own letter.

Dear Juliet, if you ever really existed, you practically stand for love itself, but I'm not sure I believe in you, or in love for that matter. I want so badly not to feel this way, but I don't know where to start.

P.S., she added with amusement, *I thought your balcony would be bigger.*

CHAPTER 6

When Sarah awoke, she had to take a long moment to remember where she was. Certainly not in her Chicago condo, she decided, listening to the low babble of sound from outside.

There were no police sirens, angry honking horns from impatient drivers, or other sounds of rush and bustle. Instead, she heard church bells tolling out the time in the distance, the quiet hum of distant traffic, and what sounded like people talking as they walked, though she couldn't understand them. Suddenly it hit her: she was in Verona!

She bounced up in bed excitedly and stretched luxuriously before sliding out from underneath the duvet. The thick drapes at the windows were still drawn, letting only a bit of the morning sun filter through. She shrugged on a fluffy bathrobe and skipped over to open the drapes, then unlatched the double doors and stepped out onto the balcony.

Immediately she was struck by the difference between this city's rush hour and a typical morning in her home city.

Here people didn't seem so hurried; they moved along as though they had places to be of course, but the general attitude seemed to be that those places would still be there, no matter what time they arrived.

People conversed in Italian as they walked, but there weren't as many cell phones as Sarah was used to, and there was little sign of the impatient, demanding tone that people seemed to use constantly in Chicago.

The attitude here in Italy was definitely much more laid-back.

She leaned over the railing a bit for a better view of the cobblestone streets below. The church bells were louder out here, echoing in the distance.

An older Italian woman with a floral scarf tied over her greying hair was selling flowers from a stall in the street, laughing and chatting with a group of women who had stopped to buy fresh flowers.

From the baskets and bags they were carrying, Sarah guessed they had made an early trip to the market for bread and vegetables and were now on their way back home.

Here and there, men and women seemed to be going to their workplaces; she spied a trio of small boys in school uniforms racing with glee through the street, weaving through the crowd, and she wondered idly if they were going to school or had just snuck out.

She heard footsteps behind her, and Nate joined her on the balcony, tying on his own bathrobe.

He took an appreciative deep breath of the warm summer air.

"*Buongiorno*, sweetheart," he said, affecting a deep Italian accent and giving Sarah a kiss. "What are you looking at?"

"Just the people," she said with a smile, leaning on the railing. "Look at them. They're so different from the crowds back home; they look so relaxed, so happy, even though they're just going about a normal day."

I wish we could capture some of that mood she thought to herself, but didn't say out loud.

Nate stayed by her elbow a moment longer, then ruffled her hair affectionately.

"Maybe it's some of that famous Italian magic," he said teasingly. "Come on now, do you want to stand in the window and gawk all day, or do you want to get out there and explore?"

Sarah smiled and stepped back inside, shutting the balcony door behind her. Maybe Nate was right; maybe there was some magic at work here, but could it work on them? Though it seemed to be having an effect already, she thought, noting how much more relaxed Nate seemed already.

CHAPTER 7

THE COUPLE DRESSED AT A LEISURELY PACE AND set out to explore their surroundings.

Sarah had been unsure about the weather, but they had lucked into a glorious June weekend with full sunshine and mild temperatures, and she soon took off her jacket and stuffed it in her shoulder bag so she could enjoy the feel of the sun on her arms.

Encouraged by the relaxed pace of the locals, they ambled along down the street, drinking in the sights, sounds and smells of the morning.

The first stop was a small café just down the street from their hotel, where Nate and Sarah ducked in to get breakfast. The middle-aged man behind the counter was enthusiastic about showing his American guests the full spread of dishes available for breakfast: cappuccinos and other hot, milky coffees; trays of *cornettos* and other pastries filled with cream, jam or chocolate; biscottis and pieces of bread; fruit salads; yoghurt; and *muesli*, which Sarah was unsure of until she realised that it was akin to granola and fruit with milk.

Her relief must have shown on her face because the man laughed gently. "Don't worry, *signora*. You might not understand all the menu items, but I think you'll find you enjoy Italian cuisine very much." He grinned. "You know, in some parts of Italy, we used to break the fast with a glass of red wine and biscuits." He laughed again at the look on Nate and Sarah's faces. "Ah, don't worry. Just *caffè e latte* and some pastries for Americans, *si*?"

In the end, Nate selected a pastry with jam and Sarah chose one full of rich chocolate, and they ordered two frothy cappuccinos as well.

Having eaten, they laid out their map of the city and guidebook and began plotting their day. Much of the city had modern roads and taxis, of course, but with the gorgeous weather, the couple hoped to spend much of their time in Verona walking, so they could better take in the sights.

Eventually, they agreed to begin their tour at one end of the city and work their way slowly across over the next two days, giving themselves plenty of time to linger anywhere they might like.

Their first stop was the Verona Arena, which according to the guidebook had been built by the Romans in 30 A.D.

"Can you just imagine," Nate said, "building something that would last all those years?" The sheer size of the stone arches was impressive, and Sarah was glad to have her camera at hand to snap a few pictures.

As they walked around the arena, she tried to imagine what it would have been like to be a spectator there when it was first built, but her imagination just wasn't up to the task—the magnitude of the place was overpowering.

"It says here that 30,000 spectators could fit inside for events," she noted, holding up the guidebook.

Nate read over her shoulder. "They still pack in quite the crowds for concerts, it seems. Twenty thousand at a time. Looks like they have a pretty impressive summer opera program, too."

Sarah shut the book, only a little disappointed. They'd spent a bit of time walking around the Arena, and she'd enjoyed it immensely, but to see a performance inside would have been breathtaking.

As if he could read her thoughts, Nate smiled a little. "Hey, we missed it this year, but maybe another year."

Really? Sarah smiled at him and flipped to another page in the guidebook. The magic of Verona, indeed.

If she'd known this city was all they needed to get Nate smiling again, she'd have flown here months ago.

CHAPTER 8

DECLAN WOKE AT DAWN AS WAS HIS HABIT, AND lay still in bed for a while as he collected his thoughts.

A church bell was tolling somewhere in the distance, but otherwise, it was quiet. He got up, dressed and went downstairs to the breakfast room of his hotel.

There was a tempting array of pastries, breads and jams, fruit and other items laid out for guests, and he selected his breakfast half-heartedly.

He had determined that morning to enjoy everything as much as possible, for the sake of Hannah's memory, even if everything he saw and did recalled her ghost.

Drinking a cappuccino reminded him of

trips to Starbucks; talking haltingly to the concierge of the hotel reminded him of how his wife could so easily strike up a conversation with any stranger at any time, while he'd never shared her gift of the gab.

Enough with that, he thought, stepping outside; he was determined if somewhat grimly, to buck up and enjoy the day.

Photography was a hobby he'd enjoyed as a teenager and in college but had later neglected, despite Hannah's urging.

It was a nice pursuit but a solo one, and he'd let his photography gear collect dust as he threw himself happily into married life and renovating their new home.

For this trip though, he thought it was fitting that he dust it off and put it to good use.

Outside his spirits lifted a bit. The morning was warming up to a pleasant temperature, the sun was shining, and the air smelled like fresh herbs and lavender from the planters around the entrance of the hotel.

Looking down the side streets full of old stone architecture and iron detailing piqued his photographer's eye, as did the groups of locals strolling through the streets.

There were younger people with cell

phones and briefcases, probably headed to work, and then there were the obvious tourists, toting cameras or day bags.

But there were also groups of people chattering rapidly in Italian—children heading to school, an older couple strolling hand in hand through the streets, a vendor with newspapers talking and laughing with a customer.

The upbeat vibe of the people around him was infectious, and Declan decided to forgo a taxi and start his day with a brisk walk to his first destination, the Verona Arena.

He took a few panorama shots to capture the scale of the amphitheatre and then spent a little time zooming in on the finer details of the architecture, noting little things like the curve of a pillar or the shadows cast by an arch.

Next, he moved on through the neighboring Piazza Bra, which was packed with tourists and locals alike.

This afforded him some excellent opportunities for people-watching, and even though he'd never considered himself a portrait photographer, he found plenty of subject matter here.

A mother and father was trying to take

pictures of their two children in front of a fountain; the boy, who looked about four, kept turning to dunk his hands in the water, prompting the mother to run forward and scold him.

He saw a family buying gelato from one of the stalls; an older man sitting on a bench feeding the pigeons; and a group of young women, probably schoolmates or old friends on holiday, setting out the contents of their picnic basket for an early morning brunch.

One young couple in particular caught his attention. They were obviously tourists, sitting on a park bench and consulting a guidebook; the man was pointing at a bronze statue in the piazza and saying something to the woman. She burst out laughing, and he pulled her closer, laughing along.

Declan studied them, feeling a wave of sadness—they reminded him so much of himself and Hannah, not long after their wedding—but he felt something else too, a little bit of inner warmth at seeing someone else so happy.

The woman laid her head on the man's shoulder, and Declan framed a perfect shot of them with the gardens in the background, and instinctively pressed the shutter button.

Though almost immediately he felt guilty; their happiness seemed like it should stay private and he felt like this was a rare moment for them, though he couldn't have said why.

CHAPTER 9

EVERYWHERE LILY WENT, SHE WATCHED THE people around her.

Slowly, her writer's mind was starting to assign backstories to the couples she saw in the street: the elderly couple on a park bench had been coming there daily for decades to feed the birds; a younger couple getting gelato from a street vendor was celebrating an anniversary with a romantic trip to this city; a pregnant young woman dining at an outdoor café was probably a local, and Lily wondered if she was impressed with the hubbub of tourists around her.

They were all looking for the most romantic locales in the city and talking endlessly about Shakespeare, something that

Lily thought must either amuse or annoy residents.

She consulted her guidebook and moved on, deciding to visit Juliet's tomb next.

It was in a small, dark garden, and even though Lily told herself firmly that no romantic heroine was actually buried here, it was certainly a moody enough place to inspire the masses.

It was also quieter than most other tourist sites she'd seen, and a good place to collect her thoughts. She was still musing when she looked at her watch and realised it was now midday; she would have to find someplace for lunch before continuing with her sightseeing.

She consulted her smartphone, looking for a list of good local cafes or trattorias where she might find a bite to eat. There was a plethora of choices, so when she returned to the street to hail a cab she asked her driver for a recommendation.

"Somewhere local? I take you to Marco and Valentina's Café Flores." He glanced at her phone. "Not on your guide list maybe, but you will not be disappointed."

Lily wasn't so sure; she couldn't find the place he mentioned in a web search. Still, she reasoned that if she disliked it she could simply find somewhere else, and directed the driver to take her there as quickly as possible.

She was quite starving.

The eatery in question was tucked away down a quiet side street, not far from the famous Casa di Giulietta but far enough that the crowds weren't humming outside the door.

It was the sort of place Lily might have walked by without a second thought. With some trepidation, she pushed open the front door and went inside, but her doubts were almost immediately dispelled.

She'd heard people describe 'stepping through a doorway into another world', but she'd never experienced it herself.

Going into the little trattoria was just such an experience.

Inside, the small restaurant was decorated in a rustic yet inviting fashion, with homey wood tables and chairs inviting diners to retire to quieter corners or group around one of the large common tables at the centre of the room.

The ceiling was low and boasted exposed wooden beams from which hung strings of lantern lights, casting a soft ambience over the room.

Old pieces of artwork, framed photographs and neatly clipped and framed newspaper articles covered the walls, and a generous wine rack at one end of the restaurant showed off a selection of local wine bottles.

It was more than just the interior décor that caught Lily's attention however; it was the atmosphere. There was music playing somewhere, but Cafe Flores still had a quiet, almost restful feel.

It felt like ... like stepping into someone's home, she decided; like going into their kitchen and feeling that you belonged there, and would be immediately served a healthy portion of delicious food and some excellent company besides.

She couldn't decide why she suddenly had that feeling but decided it must be the combo of hunger and the smell of something delicious wafting from out back.

Lily had been so caught up in her reflections that she hadn't noticed the elderly Italian man polishing glasses behind the low bar that ran along one wall. He had a healthy tan, a shock of white hair neatly combed back, and surprisingly green eyes that twinkled when she smiled at her. "*Benvenuto*! Welcome to Café Flores. I am Marco; this is my wife Valentina."

From the kitchen a woman emerged, wiping her hands on an apron. "Ah, *Benvenuto*! Sit, we will bring you lunch."

Lily wasn't used to this kind of casual dining, but she did as she was bid while the couple began bringing dishes from the kitchen. There were no menus, apparently; just a steady stream of appetisers, antipasti and side dishes, with a large decanter of wine placed at her elbow to accompany the meal.

Lily was soon surrounded by the local cuisine: cold meats and cheeses wrapped in bread; vegetables, both hot and cold; and a platter of smoked fish and chicken.

There was plenty of *bruschetta* and *zuppa* before the main dishes, and a warm smile and exclamation of "*Buon appetito!*" with each new dish laid on the table.

Finally, she sat back in her chair with a sigh. Far from being a hole-in-the-wall establishment, this little restaurant had served up one of the best meals of her life.

The couple, Marco and Valentina who owned Cafe Flores, seemed happy to sit at the common table with their guest and chat as she drank a strong espresso after dinner.

Gradually Lily learned a bit of their story: married for nearly fifty years, they had run the restaurant for most of that time, and had no plans to close any time soon.

"It's practically a part of the family," Valentina laughed, as Marco grasped her hand with a smile.

The two beamed at each other and shared a look that Lily instantly recognised: the look of two people so deeply in love that nothing could touch it.

"And what about you?" Valentina said, returning her attention to their guest. "*Ci perdoni.* We've been going on about ourselves and not asking anything about you. What brings you to Verona?"

Lily assured them that she very much enjoyed listening to them talk, and told them briefly about her job as a novelist. They nodded respectfully at that, as most people did once they found out what she did for a living.

But here in this little dining room, halfway around the world, her name in print and all of her material accomplishments didn't seem to matter so much.

"And so you are in Verona to write?" Marco prodded gently, and she hesitated.

"Yes, only ...well ...I'm just not sure where to begin. I mostly write love stories, you see ..." The couple nodded, brightening. "But I just can't seem to get my latest one started."

She didn't have the heart to tell a couple so clearly in love that it was her inner cynic making the project difficult, and not mere writer's block.

"Where better to find inspiration than a city so steeped in love?" Valentina said with a smile, and Lily smiled back.

"I suppose that's true. I was laughing at the tourists at Juliet's house earlier, but in a way, I suppose I'm just the same. I could use a touch of her guidance. For the book, and myself, I suppose."

The older couple gave each other a long look that she couldn't discern.

"And have you found it?" Valentina asked gently, and Lily laughed ruefully.

"No. I just found a lot of tourists with cameras. But I guess the romance of this city just doesn't work for me, because I'm not really feeling inspired at all."

Valentina surprised her by reaching across

the table to pat her hand. "I wouldn't give up so soon, my dear. So many people come to this city looking for different things, and they all have different ideas about love. I think perhaps you won't find it until you stop looking."

Lily considered the woman's odd remark for a moment.

Before she could think of an answer, though, Valentina stood. "But enough about serious things! Before you go looking for inspiration again, you must try my *zabaglione.* I don't believe anything difficult should be done until you've had dessert."

And with a wink and smile, the Italian woman returned once more to the kitchen.

CHAPTER 10

Sᴀʀᴀʜ ᴀɴᴅ Nᴀᴛᴇ ᴡᴀɴᴅᴇʀᴇᴅ ᴛʜʀᴏᴜɢʜ ᴛʜᴇ Piazza Bra, the pretty square adjoining the Arena. A large garden full of fragrant cedar and pine trees welcomed them, and they sat on a park bench in the shade to enjoy the scene.

The wide streets were filled with other tourists snapping photos, enjoying the gardens, or grabbing something to eat from one of the cafes.

Here the paving returned to the old cobblestone variety, and the surrounding buildings all had a rustic, time-weathered look. They were painted in weathered shades of tan, rust, yellow and beige, and most featured wrought-iron or stone balconies on the upper floors.

Small flocks of pigeons were enjoying a

leisurely mid-morning hunt for scraps left in the park by careless picnickers.

Nate pointed out the fountain in the middle of the square and a large bronze statue of a man on a horse. "The first king of Italy, Victor Emmanuel the Second. They erected the statue after his death."

"And did he do anything particular to merit a statue? Besides being a king, of course."

"Of course." Nate studied the guidebook again. "It says here that he was the first king of a united Italy since the sixth century. Oh, check out his full name, it's a mouthful: Vittorio Emanuele Maria Alberto Eugenio Ferdinando Tommaso di Savoia. You can bet that just rolled off his mama's tongue when she was mad."

Sarah burst into laughter, and after a moment Nate joined in. When the moment passed, he glanced at her and gave her a funny smile. "What?"

Sarah shrugged, unable to contain what she knew was a goofy grin. Instead, she put her head on his shoulder, and he moved an arm around her, pulling her closer to the bench. "This is nice," she said.

"What is? Mocking the birth names of dead royalty?"

"You know what I mean," she said with a grin, poking him in the side. "Us, being here, having fun. No stress." She looked up at him. "I've missed just having fun with you, like we used to."

Nate stroked her hair, looking serious. "I've missed it too. I want this vacation to be a fresh start for us."

She smiled her agreement, and he gave her a quick kiss on the nose. "Now, I don't know about you, but all this walking is making me hungry. Is that a café I see over there?"

It wasn't yet time for lunch and the place they selected wasn't particularly busy, so they bought bottles of fruit juice and *paninis*; bread rolls stuffed with salami, cheese and vegetables.

Sarah was hungrier than she'd realised though, and she ate her sandwich gratefully while they chatted with the proprietor.

"Most of the shops will close all afternoon for siesta," he explained. "If you want to do any shopping, you'll need to get it done early in the day. You can still wander around and enjoy the sights, though. Where are you headed next?"

Nate explained their plan to move across the city, hitting most of the major attractions as they did so.

He nodded. "*Si, si,* well next you'll want to visit the Castelvecchio and the museum there —you could probably spend the rest of the day there alone. And of course, explore the Skaliger Bridge and the area along the Adige River. It's beautiful there, plenty of places to take pictures, and so much history to explore. If you have extra time this week, you might even take a rafting tour of the river—you can see another side of the city that isn't apparent from the streets."

Nate and Sarah thanked him for the advice, and he moved away to help another customer. They finished their *paninis* and consulted the map for their next activity.

Nate thought that if they went on foot they would only need to walk about a mile to reach Castelvecchio, and since it wasn't quite yet noon and they were both dressed to walk, they decided to forgo the cab and go on foot.

It turned out to be a wise decision—the route to Castelvecchio was fairly straightforward, and Sarah was enjoying the chance to stretch her legs so much after the time spent in taxis, trains and aeroplanes. The guidebook listed the place as a medieval castle, and Sarah was initially a little disappointed to see that there were no four-story-high turrets or other trademark bits of architecture that she expected all castles to have.

Once they were up close, however, she quickly changed her mind. The size and majesty of the castle was in full effect, from the heavy stonework of the buildings to the towers and the adjoining bridge that spanned the Adige River.

Castelvecchio was a compact but powerfully built structure, a square compound with a minimum of decoration. It had clearly been built with defence in mind, and walking through the interior Sarah could appreciate what it might have taken to breach the walls.

Towers overlooked a now-dry moat; according to their book, it had once been filled with water from the Adige. Sarah was now well and truly impressed; the size and scale of the castle, the old brick masonry and Gothic detailing all made her feel as though she were stepping back in time.

If she ignored the hum of the tourists around her, she could almost imagine that she was a heroine in a medieval tale, waiting in the castle for a prince to bring news of approaching armies.

Much of Verona had been damaged by air raids and bombing during the Second World War, and so much of the original architecture and appearance of the city had been patched over during rebuilding. Somehow though, Castelvecchio had more or less retained its original appearance, for which Sarah was grateful. It seemed right somehow that such an old and majestic building should soldier on through the years, even if it were no longer needed to house armies.

The couple spent nearly three hours exploring the castle, the bridge and the museum, which housed a variety of sculptures, paintings and frescoes from the fourteenth century.

By the time they left the castle, they were ready for their lunch meal and soon found a cute little trattoria where they ordered pasta with tomatoes and pesto, chicken caprese, fresh-baked bread and delicious local red wine.

Nate and Sarah lingered over their meal, finally admitting to each other that they were too full even to order gelato for dessert. "Maybe later," Sarah groaned. "I'm too full of pasta to eat another bite."

Outside the afternoon was once again

dusky and they decided to make one last stop before returning to their hotel. The Gavi Arch was not far from Castelvecchio and the trattoria where they'd dined, so they decided to walk there to enjoy the view in the late evening.

Sarah leaned her head sleepily on his arm. Nate pointed out a picture in the guidebook that showed the Arch at night, illuminated and shining next to the river. "Why don't we come back tonight to see it?"

"Sounds like a plan," said Sarah, checking her watch. "I vote we catch a cab back to the hotel and take a nap first. Then we can go out for dinner and more sightseeing."

"We could do that," Nate said amiably, hailing a taxi. He paused and gave her a pointed look. "Or..."

She looked at him for a moment before breaking into a grin of her own. *Or,* she thought as they settled into the taxi, *we could just stay in...*

CHAPTER 11

MOVING ON FROM THE PIAZZA, DECLAN bought more cappuccino and a sandwich roll from a small kiosk and decided to walk the short distance to the old Castelvecchio, a medieval castle and bridge spanning the Adige River.

It was an impressive structure, low and heavy with a series of towers that had obviously once been perfect for shooting arrows or cannons at an oncoming enemy.

He thought that Hannah would have appreciated the imposing build of the structure and the tactical design, complete with a moat (now dry) and a bridge to thwart intruders.

The courtyard of the castle was sunny and well-tended as a garden, but inside it was cool and darker, and the medieval feeling was well-preserved.

Declan wandered a bit through the old stone interior, peering out the slotted windows and snapping pictures of the Gothic architectural details.

There weren't as many tourists inside as there were outside, so he had plenty of chances to shoot without people entering the frame.

He felt like he'd found a portal to the Verona of Shakespeare's time, and he could see how a writer would find inspiration for a tale of warring families in the city—clearly the early Italians who lived here put a high priority on defence. The castle was not built to be easily overrun.

Once he was finished in the dim interior, he moved out to the bridge; a low, heavy stone structure spanning the river, punctuated by defensible spots for archers and military men to fend off an enemy.

Though it looked as though it had seen better days—Declan noted sadly a bit of graffiti as he walked—and his guidebook informed him that much of the reconstruction throughout Verona was the result of damage sustained during the Second World War.

Still, even if the bridge wasn't in a pristine state, it provided ample angles for new photos, and Declan could easily imagine standing here in a prior century.

Next, he took a taxi to the famous Casa di Giulietta and joined the tourists buying tickets at the entrance.

He could see some of the attractions of the house; it was a well-preserved example of a medieval Italian home, and the interior had been turned into a tidy museum chronicling Verona's life in the thirteenth and fourteenth centuries.

There were elaborate costumes throughout, which he gathered were from a film about Romeo and Juliet, and examples of medieval art and sculpture.

He took a few pictures before he returned to the courtyard to photograph the balcony.

From his position standing on the stones, it didn't look like much. It was only a simple stone balcony, nothing more. How interesting, he thought, that something so basic could fire the imagination of so many people.

Once again a few tourists asked him to take pictures as they posed in front of the balcony or with the statue of Juliet that stood watching mournfully over the courtyard.

He obliged, before wandering to the wall where lovers left their letters to Juliet.

He thought about the kind of thing he would write.

How do I pick up the threads of my life? Is it even possible?

He wasn't sure that this was the sort of letter most people would stuff in the wall though. He saw mostly younger women who were probably writing about boyfriends who had left them unhappily alone.

So Declan composed another letter, this one to the lovelorn letter writers:

Love doesn't have to make sense, to make sense.

CHAPTER 12

As he tucked the note into a crevice on the wall, he could almost picture Hannah on Juliet's balcony, dramatically clutching her chest and spouting a line or two of Shakespeare.

The image made him smile.

Then, checking his watch he decided to make one last stop at a nearby tourist attraction, the Gavi Arch, before stopping for lunch.

The Arch had once stood as an entrance to Verona but had been dismantled by the French during Napoleon's time, and the ruins had sat in the Piazza for some time before being constructed in the 1930s.

It too bore graffiti marks and obvious signs of age, but it was an impressive structure nonetheless and Declan spent a little time looking for the best angles of the structure with his camera.

Finally, he packed away his gear and set off in search of a good place to grab a bite.

He was a little surprised by how much he was enjoying himself; for a moment he felt a little guilty as he realised with a start that he was thinking less of how much he missed Hannah.

For a moment he stopped walking, feeling almost ashamed of himself; how could he enjoy this trip at all without constantly mourning her?

Then it slowly came to him that he was thinking only of what she would say or do if she was at his elbow, the little remarks she would make about the historical sites he'd visited or the silly poses she might adopt, standing at an archer's post in the castle or on the bridge.

No, he wasn't mourning her loss, but he wasn't forgetting her, either.

In a way, Declan felt as though she were not far away.

The words from her letter came back to him:

I think once you're there in Verona you'll feel me with you, at least in spirit. And I hope all the love you sense there will help you to feel whole again.

He *did* feel more whole than he had all year since her passing.

Was it the busy itinerary he'd set for himself or was there *really* something about this place that worked its way into the soul?

CHAPTER 13

Saturday morning dawned just as sunny and beautiful as the previous day, but Sarah and Nate slept late and took their time getting ready to head out into the city.

After their little afternoon siesta the evening before, they ended up going out for dinner and wine, then a bit of nighttime sight-seeing, and then more wine.

It was the first time in months that Sarah could remember them fully relaxing and enjoying themselves without bickering about something petty.

She just hoped the feeling lasted.

Finally, they dressed and ate, and pulled out the guidebook for day two of their adventure.

Sarah was adamant that they visit the famed

Casa di Giulietta, supposedly the house that the famous Juliet Capulet had once lived in. There, visitors could leave letters in Juliet's Wall, where the lovelorn placed notes seeking advice on unrequited love and other romantic problems.

The couple caught a taxi outside their hotel and soon landed amid a throng of tourists, all taking advantage of a gorgeous Saturday morning to snap photos and reenact their favourite scenes from Shakespeare's drama.

Sarah had enjoyed reading *Romeo and Juliet* in school, but she wasn't so enamoured with the story that she was going to pose on a balcony and recite lines from the play in front of a crowd of strangers.

She contented herself with exploring the house and the grounds. The house and Juliet's famous balcony overlooked a stone courtyard that was packed with tourists. Tall narrow windows with iron detailing on the frames overlooked the cobblestones where Romeo supposedly stood to court his beloved.

The last of the summer greenery brightened the shadows of the courtyard and helped distract from some of the small concessions to

modern times, like electric lamps on the courtyard walls.

Inside the house, care had been taken to
restore the interior to something resembling a
medieval state. The floors were a mix of well-
trod wood and colourful large tiles, but the
ceiling was beautiful: a design of large tiles,
painted with flowers in shades of red, yellow
and green.

At one point the crowd of tourists in the
house thinned out a bit, and Sarah stole back to
the balcony. She wasn't going to do anything
silly for a tourist picture, but she wanted to at
least stand on the balcony for a moment.

Even if the cynics were right (and they
usually were, she reflected) and this house had
never belonged to the real-life counterparts to
the Capulets, it was wonderful to pretend that
the story was true and a lovestruck young girl
had once stood here and professed her love for
the boy she couldn't have.

As Sarah stood on the balcony surveying
the courtyard, she caught sight of Nate leaning
against a wall in the corner. He wasn't that
interested in the house itself and decided to
stay outside in the sun and relax. As she
watched him she had a sudden panicky

thought: what if all the cheer and easy-going humour they were experiencing here in Verona faded as soon as they got back home?

What if the return of the old spark between them dissipated once they were away from the romance of Italy and back in the grind of a day-to-day routine, complete with the stress of jobs, bills to pay and families to deal with? She thought of her parents' deep dislike for Nate and his family, and dread swelled afresh in her chest.

Just then Nate looked up and saw her on the balcony. His face lit up in a grin, and he waved to her. Sarah smiled and waved back. She didn't want to let her pangs of doubt ruin the rest of this weekend, and as for whatever came afterwards… she would just have to find a way to deal with it then.

Slowly she picked her way back through the house and out to the courtyard. Nate put an arm around her; he was warm from standing in the sun, and she breathed deeply of his aftershave.

"How was the house?" he asked.

"Beautiful." She described the interior. "If you try hard enough, you can almost imagine Juliet standing there on the balcony."

Nate squinted hard at the building. "I guess I don't have your imagination," he confessed, "because to me it just looks like an empty balcony. But I'm glad you're having fun."

"I am," she said happily. "Come on, I want to look at the wall before we go."

Juliet's Wall was where heartbroken people left letters to Juliet, asking for her advice on unrequited love and all other romantic dilemmas.

Sarah vaguely recalled reading a newspaper article about the women who called themselves "the secretaries of Juliet" and took it upon themselves to collect, read and answer the letters. Apparently, it was a bit of an old tradition, and she was impressed that anyone would devote so much time to the task. It couldn't be easy, dealing with heartbreak on a daily basis.

Sarah stood gazing at the wall awhile, thinking about everything she would say if she wrote a letter and placed it there.

Dear Juliet, I'm so afraid my marriage is doomed to fail. So many things seem to go wrong, and I always worry about what the next thing will be. Help me turn back the clock so Nate and I can be happy again.

She was stirred from her thoughts by a touch on the elbow.

Nate was looking at his watch. "Are you hungry? While you were inside I was chatting with one of the site caretakers, and they recommended a little trattoria just down the street. We could get lunch before we do any more sightseeing."

Sarah was surprised to see that it was now well past one. "I hadn't realised it was so late. Yes, I'm starving. Let's grab a bite and then we'll decide where to go next."

CHAPTER 14

CAFÉ FLORES WAS ONLY A FEW SHORT BLOCKS away from the hustle and bustle at Juliet's house, but it might as well have been on the other side of the city for the change in atmosphere.

Tucked away on a quiet side street and with only a small sign to advertise its presence, the little trattoria was like a spot of calm in the busy sea of tourists flooding the city.

Nate and Sarah found themselves there with a handful of other lunchtime diners, all grouped around a common table in the rustic interior.

The couple lingered over dinner, ordering dish after dish; risotto, pasta, vegetables, and meats, all with plenty of bread and wine on the side. There was a delicious custard and cups of strong hot espresso for dessert, after which the other diners slowly began to drift away.

Nate and Sarah lingered on, enjoying the relaxed ambience and not eager to rush on with their day.

After a while, the owners came out and sat down at the table with them. The man who was called Marco introduced himself to Nate and struck up a conversation about the military history of Verona.

Valentina began chatting with Sarah about the day's sightseeing at Juliet's house and suggested they go into the back room of the restaurant to retrieve a book she had discussing the history of Romeo and Juliet's story in Verona.

After the two women had left the front room, Marco paused and looked at Nate.

"You two are recently married?"

Nate answered in the affirmative and explained that the trip was supposed to be a sort of belated honeymoon. "We've been having some problems," he said falteringly. "Sometimes it seems like we just weren't fated to be together."

The older man thought about that for a

moment. "So many people who come to this city mix up love and fate. Fated to be together, fated to be torn apart. *Ma no*, it is not so. To put such a thing as love into the hands of chance," here he shook his head, "it is foolishness. Love is made. You have to work for it."

"I've tried," Nate said doubtfully, "or...I think I have. But even so, I know her family doesn't like me. They don't think I'm good enough for her."

"She must think you're good enough for her, she married you," Marco clapped the younger man on the back. "Maybe you need to think back to the time when you first met. Think about all the things you saw in each other that made you fall in love. And don't let anyone else's opinion get in the way."

In the storeroom, Valentina was pulling a dog-eared book from a shelf and handing it to Sarah, who thanked her with the little Italian she'd picked up from her guidebook.

"*Grazie*," she said, putting the book in her bag, and Valentina smiled.

"I think you'll enjoy it. You're a newlywed?"

"Yes, this summer. We were supposed to

HOLLY GREENE

take our honeymoon in Indonesia..." She struggled to think of a good, condensed explanation of their troubles over the past several months, but Valentina intervened with a knowing look.

"Life interferes. Sometimes it ruins our plans. But you can't allow these problems to alter your path. They're just hills that need to be climbed, that's all."

Sarah smiled a little. "I try to tell myself that, but I still worry."

"About what?"

"That Nate and I won't work out. Everything's just been so bumpy since we got married," she suddenly burst out. It felt good to confess her frustrations to someone. "My family nags and nags, and sometimes Nate can seem flippant about things, like he just wants to sit back and let them happen. I love him and I don't want to lose him, but it seems like we have a little spark of something and then it fades. And sometimes I don't know what to do."

Valentina considered this for a long moment, and Sarah began to feel embarrassed for telling her troubles to this complete stranger.

Then the older woman spoke slowly.

84

"Sometimes it's hard to see the good in things, especially when times are rough. But those are the times you have to try especially hard to hold onto the good, and to see all the good in the person you love. You might not like them very much," and she laughed a little, "but hold onto those good thoughts. Even a small spark can be kept alive if you keep fanning it, and it can become a very large fire. It just needs that care and attention."

Sarah turned over this thought in her mind. Valentina smiled and patted her arm. "Come, I've kept you away from your husband too long. You two should go out and enjoy a bit more of Verona. How long will you be here?"

"Not much longer, unfortunately," Sarah said as they reentered the main room. Marco was lounging casually at the table, drinking a glass of wine; Nate looked lost deep in thought.

He shook his head and stood up when he saw her. "Are you ready to move on?"

"Yes," she said, giving his hand a quick squeeze. He smiled, still looking distracted.

Valentina came to stand beside Marco, who wrapped an arm around her waist and looked up at her, and the two exchanged a smile.

"Come by again before you leave," Marco

said. "We'll make sure to have fresh *zabaglione* waiting for you."

The younger couple agreed to try to return to the trattoria before leaving the city, and Valentina smiled at Sarah as if to say: *And remember what we talked about.*

CHAPTER 15

Nate and Sarah decided that their next stop would be Juliet's tomb since it seemed to be a less-visited tourist attraction and they wanted to escape the crowds for a bit.

The crypt was located in the garden of an older house that had been converted into a museum, and they were the only visitors ducking through the house and lingering by the silent grave. Sarah knit her brow in thought.

"It's really sad when you think about it, right? They could have had a happy life together. Instead, they died before they could even get started."

Nate hugged her, propping his chin on her shoulder as he spoke. She thought he seemed distant. "They probably felt so pressured by everyone around them. Everyone remembers their story being so romantic, but I wonder if they ever had any doubts."

Sarah turned to face him. *Do you ever have doubts about us?* she wanted to blurt out, but the words seemed too big for the tiny garden, and she held them back. Instead, she said lightly, "Well, this place is making me feel morbid. Let's move on somewhere else."

Nate was still quiet as they left the museum. They decided to visit some of the churches in Verona, which were famous for their marble sculptures and exquisite interiors, before returning to their hotel for the night. As they walked through the cool interiors, footsteps echoing on the marble floors, Sarah thought that she'd only ever seen cathedrals like this in movies or on the travel channel. She had to crane her neck back to see the paintings and coloured glass high up on the walls and set into the ceilings. The churches were filled with a mix of tourists and worshippers, and the couple moved quietly through the buildings, murmuring respectfully as they went.

All the while Sarah thought that Nate

seemed as though he was moving on autopilot, thinking about something else entirely.

When they finally decided to call it a day, the sun was setting over Verona, lighting up the red clay rooftops and the trees on distant hilltops. The air was growing brisk with the evening, and they happily took a taxi back to the hotel.

Sarah sat on the bed and slowly brushed out her hair while Nate flipped through the TV channels, looking for something mindless to watch as they relaxed. She was sad that they only had one day left in the city; she'd so enjoyed their time together but couldn't help feeling doubtful about their return trip.

She wondered if Nate felt the same way but couldn't bring herself to ask him.

They'd had such a relaxing 48 hours, laughing, dining and enjoying each other's company; the last thing she wanted now was to spoil it by starting an awkward conversation when they were both tired.

Nate finally turned off the TV. "Did you have anything in particular you wanted to do tomorrow?"

"Not really," she said, slipping into bed and turning off the bedside lamp. "You?"

"I have some ideas," he said, but wouldn't elaborate when she asked him. "It's a surprise. If I told you then the surprise would be ruined."

"Is it a good surprise?" she asked hopefully, and he nodded and kissed her. "Get some sleep. I want our last day here to be the best."

"Me too," she said, content. Yes, she would fan that spark of hope, even if it took all her energy. With that thought in her mind, Sarah curled her body against her husband's and fell happily asleep.

CHAPTER 16

Declan decided to just walk through the city on impulse and see what might pop up for his camera.

He spent a great deal of time in the piazzas, photographing the crowds and the medieval architecture. There were some elaborate tombs to visit and amazing cathedrals, complete with gorgeous frescoes and sculptures inside. Where he could take his camera, he shot frame after frame and where he couldn't he tucked it politely away and soaked it all in with his eyes.

The churches in Verona left him awe-struck, and he felt it would be difficult to fully capture their scale on film, but he tried his best to do them justice. The spires, stained glass windows, arches and pillars afforded him countless close-up and panoramic shots.

He marvelled over the huge marble entrance to the Duomo di Verona and read with interest some of the guide signs about the history of the architecture in the churches, dating back to the twelfth century or even earlier.

It was late-afternoon when he returned to his hotel to download more photos, that he realised he'd barely eaten all day as he raced through the city, trying to capture everything he could.

He was having... *fun*, a word he hadn't used to describe his own activities in a long long time.

As he spent time exploring Verona, Declan was beginning to understand why Hannah had developed such a strong fascination with the city.

It wasn't simply that the place was full of interesting history or amazing architecture, though there was plenty of that to be certain.

It was something more: a palpable mood, a feeling that could be discerned from the crowds of people strolling through the city. So many of the people who had come here for a holiday did so with *amore* on the mind, and the collective feelings of love and optimism could be strongly felt.

Several times as Declan made his way across the city he was stopped by tourists who noticed his camera bag and asked him to take their pictures, handing off their cameras and arranging themselves hurriedly in front of some famous monument or view.

He never minded; he was happy to look through the viewfinder and see so many happy couples and families, hastily arranging scarves and hair and jackets and grinning for the camera. There was an irrepressible spirit of joy in the air and it was seeping into his bones.

CHAPTER 17

When Declan was ready for an evening meal, he decided to seek out a trattoria recommended to him by the hotel, and see what made it so special.

He was not disappointed when he arrived on the doorstep of Café Flores.

The smell of freshly cooked meats and breads wafted into the street and mixed with the warm air, and he breathed appreciatively as he entered. The owners greeted him with gusto; he was part of a small afternoon crowd enjoying platters of grilled fish, steam vegetables, pasta with a thick meat sauce, and plenty of bruschetta.

Wine was being served in large decanters and there was a small array of tempting desserts, including custard and gelato, served along with strong hot coffee to end the meal. Declan was in no rush with his meal and lingered after the other diners paid and left, hoping to chat with the owners about the city.

He wasn't disappointed. Dessert found the proprietors Marco and Valentina sharing coffee with him at a corner table. He told them about some of the places in Verona that he'd photographed thus far, including the medieval castles and elaborate cathedrals.

"And what brought you to Verona?" Marco asked, and slowly Declan related the story of Hannah, his promise, and her death. The words came clumsily at first and then started to pour out of him unbidden.

He had spent so long trying not to dwell too much on his pain, and it felt good to tell the entire story from beginning to end.

The older couple were very patient listeners, and they sat quietly until the end, only nodding in places as they listened.

"And that's how I ended up here," Declan finished, taking a breath to steady himself.

Valentina murmured sympathetically, "You're feeling a bit odd, being here without her?"

"Yes," he said sadly. "It comes and goes in waves, really. But I can't help feeling a little guilty at times. It's so hard. I know I need to find a way to move forward with my life, but I don't want to let go of her. And sometimes I realise that I'm not thinking of her often enough, and I worry that I'm forgetting her too quickly."

Marco shook his head. "You can move forward but not leave her behind. You can keep her in your heart," he explained, seeing the younger man's puzzled expression.

"You will always have your memories of her to cherish, and you should keep those close. But I don't think she would want to see you stuck in the past, being unhappy and dwelling on what could have been. I think she'd want you to move forward with your life and enjoy it. It's no slight to the dead to enjoy being alive; in a way enjoying this trip is one of the best ways you can honour her memory. You can picture her beside you one last time. I think she intended you to find some closure that way."

"I think you're right," Declan said slowly. "Before she died she wrote me a letter explaining that I would come to love this city as much as she did and that the love here would make me feel better. And I think she was right. I feel like she's here with me. Seeing so many people so happy and in love is healing, somehow."

Valentina nodded. "Love doesn't die and fade away just because a person does. You can feel their love all around you in the world when you see others in love. You feel the pain of your own loss, but it's tempered with joy for other people who are so happy. You can't really start to heal if you're only dwelling on the loss; you have to look at all the love still in the world and embrace it. There's too much out there to close your heart and remain in the past with sorrow."

All three of them sat awhile longer, Declan ruminating on her words, the couple wisely remaining quiet.

He thought about everything he'd seen during his short stay and Hannah's words to him:

I hope all the love you sense there will help you to feel whole again.

He was starting to feel, perhaps not entirely whole, but at least partially formed. He no longer felt as though he couldn't find the pieces of his own broken heart. He felt that there was a chance at being happy again, and it would be no crime to enjoy life.

The night was settling in over Verona when Declan finally thanked the couple for their time and left. As he passed out the door, however, a thought struck him, and he hastily returned. "Would you mind very much if I took a few pictures of your trattoria?" he asked, holding up the camera. "I'm sure I can't do it justice, but I'd like to try."

The couple said that of course, they'd be flattered, and Declan moved around the main room, taking a few wide shots and a few close-ups of interesting details—bottles, dishes, art on the walls. Finally, he thanked them again and left, walking slowly along the city streets toward the main thoroughfare.

He hailed a cab and returned to his hotel. Lying on the bed in his street clothes, he thought about everything he'd seen and done.

It had been a very long time since he'd lingered on thoughts of Hannah without feeling sorrow.

But since visiting Juliet's famed love letters wall, he felt a strange glow of happiness and mentally went back through all of their happiest moments together.

There was an early one of Hannah, arriving to one of their first dates in a dress and trainers. She'd never been a pretentious woman and she refused to wear high heels just to impress a date if she knew she wouldn't be comfortable. That down-to-earth attitude was one of the things that had made him fall in love with her, to begin with.

Later memories summoned a disastrous road trip that had ended with a broken-down car on the side of the road and a night spent in a cheap B&B waiting for the car to be repaired so they could go on; Hannah had somehow not been fazed in the least by this interruption to their vacation, and he thought that their night in the rundown B&B had been more relaxing than a stay at a five-star hotel.

He continued mentally flicking through a camera reel of memories: Hannah on their wedding day, finally bowing to pressure from her mother to wear 'proper' shoes, but kicking them off under her dress before their first dance and winking at him as she pressed her bare toes onto the tips of his shoes on the dance floor. Hannah, whipping up dinner for friends in the tiny kitchen of their first apartment. Hannah, with paint on her nose and a roller in one hand, dithering over two shades of yellow as she painted the dining room of their newly purchased home.

That was where Declan stopped. He wouldn't dwell on the sad memories, only on the happy ones. From now on, he would remember his wife as she was—warm, laughing, tousle-haired but still smiling when she woke in the morning—and hold those memories close as he drifted off to sleep.

For once he wasn't drifting off as an escape, but with a smile on his lips.

Love doesn't have to make sense to make sense

...

CHAPTER 18

LILY SPENT THE FOLLOWING DAY DOING SOME more light sightseeing, shopping and dining before returning to her hotel.

She filled the generous bathtub with hot water and her favourite vanilla bubble bath, poured a glass of red wine, and settled in to enjoy her bath and ponder her day.

For some strange reason, she felt compelled to return to Juliet's home, though she couldn't say why; perhaps she could find some inspiration there on a second outing.

With that hope firmly in her mind (and still no sliver of a plot forming for her book), a little while later she dressed, hailed a cab and returned to the crowded courtyard once again.

If it was possible, there were even more

tourists this evening than the last time, and Lily contented herself with finding a semi-quiet corner from which she could quietly observe.

People flowed around her, chattering in English, Italian and languages she couldn't identify. Many were taking pictures, and once again there was a steady flow of young women on Juliet's balcony, pretending to swoon as they quoted from Shakespeare's play.

Lily spent a little time studying Juliet's wall, where more letters peeked from cracks and on a whim, she slid one piece of paper out and read the words written on it.

Love doesn't have to make sense to make sense.

All around her people flowed, thinking of their own lives and loves, oblivious to her.

This simple pronouncement plus the wise words of the woman in the trattoria rattled through her head all at once, and Lily suddenly understood.

She had been searching for the perfect one-size-fits-all plot, but she was guilty of searching for the same thing in her love life.

She'd spent years chasing her version of a star-struck romance, something perfect and amazing that would fall out of the sky and into her lap, perfectly formed. Too many experiences with the bitter aftertaste of love gone sour had left her sure that no such thing existed.

But watching these couples around her was opening her eyes to the quiet strokes of love that she'd always ignored. The elderly husband was helping his wife to her feet, embracing her as she stood with some effort. Lily wondered how long they'd been married; the look of tender devotion on the man's face made her smile.

The young couple sharing gelato looked like they had probably had to scrape together the money for the trip, but whatever struggles they'd had to make it to Italy, they were clearly enjoying every minute of their visit. Even a simple ice cream was apparently an event for them. Lily thought that there must be something about love that could turn even small things into big, lovely things.

The pregnant woman at the café turned with an expectant smile as a man came up to her and leaned down to kiss her. His hand went to her belly, and they both smiled as they chatted, he rubbing her stomach and seeming to inquire about her food. He was clearly concerned for her happiness, and whatever answer she gave to his questions seemed to please him, because he bounded away and returned a moment later to her table with dessert and coffee. He seemed happy to dote on her, hovering protectively as she ate.

All around her, Lily could feel a sense of love that had nothing to do with romantic plots or grand gestures, but simply everyday life and small touches that said *I love you* without speaking a word.

She still felt a touch of envy for these happy couples, but Lily no longer found a sting of bitterness in her heart as she watched them.

Instead, she only felt a kind of happiness for them, as though by watching them she felt some of their happiness for herself.

CHAPTER 19

IT WAS LATE IN THE DAY WHEN SHE FINALLY returned to her hotel, the beginnings of a plot forming in her mind.

She wasn't sure exactly when it had occurred to her; only that it was now beating at the walls of her brain, dying to get out and onto paper.

In her room, she turned off her cell phone, switched on her laptop, and began to type.

She worked for several hours without stopping. Finally, when she was too tired to write any longer, she fell into bed and slept.

The next day she tackled her manuscript once more with enthusiasm. By that afternoon she was happy with what she'd created so far, and she stretched happily as she stood up from her writing desk and paced around the hotel room. She still had a lot of material to create, but at least she was on the right track.

Lily decided to celebrate this small victory with an early dinner out, and after changing into something more appropriate for the evening she found herself seated once again in Café Flores, watching other customers with new-found interest.

She found herself wanting to ask all of them for their stories.

Valentina had been right; as long as she was doggedly looking for her idea of a "perfect" romance, she couldn't find it.

And thanks to one of Juliet's letters, now that she was letting go of some of her assumptions, Lily saw love everywhere.

It was a couple at a corner table, enjoying an easy silence as they ate. They didn't need a ton of words to express their happiness at being together for a meal; Lily smiled a little as she saw the man take his companion's hand and tenderly bring it to his lips.

At another table, she saw a younger couple —probably on a first or very early date, she decided, from his nervousness. He was obviously trying to impress the young woman across from him, and by her coquettish laugh, Lily guessed he was probably being successful.

All around her other couples smiled, laughed and talked as they ate. Harsh lighting was absent in the restaurant in favour of candles at the tables, and the soft glow of candlelight made everything look even cosier.

Lily took another sip of her wine as she considered the dinner menu. Suddenly there was a collective gasp from the crowd, and she craned her neck to get a better look in the direction of the sound.

The nervous young man, whom she'd assumed was on a first date, was now on the floor on one knee, holding out a ring to his date. She was crying softly and nodding, unable to speak. All through the restaurant people began applauding as the young man stood and swept up his now-fiancée for a kiss.

It was the sort of scene that would have made Lily roll her eyes not that long ago, but somehow here—in this old city, surrounded by candlelight and the smell of Italian flavours—it seemed so perfect. She found it hard to come up with a cynical thought about two people who were clearly so excited about each other. Before she might have said, "Just wait and see," Now she simply thought: *Love doesn't have to make sense to make sense...*

CHAPTER 20

DECLAN WOKE UP EARLY AND REFRESHED.

He heard cathedral bells tolling in the distance and hummed a tune to himself as he dressed and ate breakfast. It took him a little while to finish moving his photos from the camera card to the laptop, editing through the pictures as he went, but once he was done he was ready to set out for the day and finish his sight-seeing.

His next stop was one he'd intended to visit earlier until he'd been sidetracked by his photo excursions.

The Lamberti Tower offered him an excellent near-aerial view of Verona, and he was happy to arrive when there were few other tourists in attendance.

Looking out over the city gave him a feeling of being somehow removed from the fray, able to observe in peace.

Here he finally did something he'd been meaning to do since he opened Hannah's letter.

In his coat pocket was a tiny bag. He was pretty sure anyone official connected with the tower would disapprove of his actions, but it was only a handful, so he didn't feel too bad.

It was his way of giving a piece of his love back to the city.

He thought Hannah would have liked to know that at least a handful of her ashes had been scattered in the city of her dreams.

He sprinkled out the ashes into his palm and let the wind take them away.

This, then, was the end; the closure he'd needed.

Other tourists were coming up the stairs to the top of the tower, and Declan took one last long look at the city. It was approaching sunset, and long shadows fell between the buildings and darkened the streets.

People were going to dinner; street vendors were closing down their stalls and heading home for the evening. The rooftops glowed reddish in the warm light, a contrast to the cool blue shadows down below.

As Declan turned to walk away he realised he recognised a man and woman who'd just come up the stairs. It was the couple on the bench he'd felt guilty for photographing in the Piazza Bra the other day.

Realising that perhaps fate was smiling on him, and still feeling energised by what he'd just done, he decided to approach them.

"Excuse me," he said to the man, who looked to be in his early thirties, with sandy hair and an American accent.

Introducing himself to the couple, Declan explained that he'd seen them a few days earlier at the piazza and couldn't help snapping their picture.

"You reminded me of something," he admitted somewhat sheepishly, surprised he was being so forthright with complete strangers. "I hope you don't mind?" he added quickly in case he sounded stalkerish. "If you give me an e-mail address I can send you the photo."

The American couple assured him that they didn't mind in the least, and the woman sought out a scrap of paper in her bag on which she jotted down her e-mail.

"Are you visiting Verona alone, or with friends?" the man asked him casually.

For a moment Declan's face shuttered. "Alone," he said, trying to smile. "My wife...died last year. She'd always wanted to visit this city. I'm visiting all the landmarks she would have wanted to see. I miss her."

He wasn't sure what it was about this city that allowed him to talk freely about his wife and his feelings but as Declan bade the couple goodbye and slowly walked down the stairs and exited the tower, his heart felt light.

He took a taxi back to his hotel, packed up his camera gear, and stretched out in bed to sleep.

That night he dreamed of Hannah, and in all of his dreams, they roamed the streets of Verona together.

When he woke in the morning he didn't feel sad; he only felt the joy of what they'd shared, and finally, a sense of peace.

As Hannah predicted, Verona had indeed worked her magic.

CHAPTER 21

LILY EVENTUALLY LEFT CAFE FLORES VERY FULL of delicious food (and probably too much wine, she admitted to herself) and ready to sleep.

She was waiting for a taxi outside when she noticed one of the trattoria couples she'd been observing, also waiting.

The woman glanced her way a couple of times, whispered something to her companion, then shyly approached.

"Excuse me," she said in an American accent, "but I had to say hello. You're Lily Forbes the writer, aren't you?"

Another time she might have felt irritated at being approached, but now she smiled warmly and nodded.

The woman looked delighted. "I'm Sarah.

And that's my husband over there. I'm a huge fan of your books."

Lily thanked her. "But I hope you're not spending all of your time here in Verona reading?" she said, with a pointed glance at Nate, and Sarah blushed.

"We're sort of on a belated honeymoon. It's been really lovely. And what about you? Are you here on vacation, or for research?"

Lily thought the other woman looked a bit hopeful, and she saw no harm in confirming the theory. "I came here to get inspiration for my next book. But to be honest, the city has changed so many of my assumptions about romance. I've learned a lot about love. It's been an eye-opener. I couldn't have picked a better place to spend my weekend."

Sarah looked curious. "I thought romance novelists were instinctively experts on love and romance?"

Lily thought about that for a second. Taxis were queuing up and the man was waving to his wife.

"Love doesn't have to make sense to make sense" she replied with a knowing smile. "Keep that in mind—a book might have a lot of fireworks, but even those die over time. The real thing is worth all the extra work it might take."

With that they parted, the young couple climbing into a cab and speeding away.

Lily would spend a few more days in Italy before returning home for work, but she already knew that she would be doing things very differently once she got back to London.

No more looking for a fireworks to land in her lap; she was going to stop chasing that ideal and start working on a real, down-to-earth romance.

And if she couldn't find the perfect relationship? She wasn't going to waste time lamenting singledom. She had so many other things in life to do—like finish her brand new novel for one.

And when it was complete, Lily knew exactly who would receive the first copy.

CHAPTER 22

SARAH WOKE UP EARLY TO FIND THAT NATE WAS already up and trying to stealthily dress and leave the room without her noticing.

She fumbled for the clock on her bedside table. "What time is it?"

"Early," he whispered, tiptoeing over to her and tucking the duvet around her shoulders. "Go back to sleep. I set the alarm for you. I'll be back soon."

"Okay," she mumbled, too sleepy to ask questions about where he was going, and she rolled over into a cloud of dreams.

When she woke a little later to the quiet chirp of the alarm clock, she realised that Nate still had not returned to the room. He'd pulled open the drapes at the windows and the balcony door, and early morning sunshine was filtering softly through the windows. Propping herself up one elbow, she noticed that he'd left a handwritten note by the alarm clock.

Arise, fair sun, it read, *and go out on the balcony. Your Romeo has a surprise for you.*

Sleepiness forgotten, Sarah tumbled out of bed and pulled on her robe in a hurry. Running across the room, she flung open the doors to the balcony and rushed outside. A flutter of wings startled her, and she looked up just in time to see a flock of pigeons whirl past her head and up onto the rooftops. She looked down over the railing to see Nate standing in the empty street, looking absurdly pleased with himself. "I couldn't get a hold of doves," he explained happily, "but I found a local boy who helped me with the pigeons. Are you surprised?"

"Very!" she laughed. "Is that why you were up so early?"

"That's part of it," he said. "Go back inside. I'll meet you in the room."

Sarah grinned and turned back inside, latching the door. She gasped in surprise. She'd been so excited about the note on the table that she hadn't even noticed a full bouquet of red roses sitting in a vase on the dresser. She picked up a note sitting next to them that read, *A rose by any other name would smell as sweet, but luckily for me, they didn't have another name in Italian, so it was easy to find these at a local shop. I know how much you love them.*

The door opened and Nate entered the room. Sarah moved across and jumped into his arms for a hug. "I love them! Why all the romantic surprises so suddenly?"

He hugged her tightly. "Because I've been thinking about us, and I realise I've goofed up a lot over the past few months. I've taken too much for granted, including our relationship. I've been too content to sit back and let things play out. But I'm not content to do that anymore. I love you, Sarah Parker, and I want to make sure you know it every minute of every day, no matter what's happening around us and no matter how crappy things seem at times. I don't want to lose this feeling we've had all weekend just because we go back home and go back to reality."

Sarah snuggled into his shoulder, her heart brimming full of emotion. "I've made mistakes too. I worry too much about everything that could go wrong, instead of focusing on what's going right. I'm going to change that."

They stood for a moment, locked in an embrace, and then Nate suddenly let go and looked at his watch with an exclamation. "Not to rush you, my dearest darling, but you'd better get ready for the day. I have a full itinerary planned, and it starts in an hour."

That was all the motivation Sarah needed to hurry through dressing and grab her day bag. Nate had already made a stop at a café and picked up pastries and cappuccinos to go; they ate quickly and caught a cab to take them across town. Sarah looked excitedly out the window as they drove. "Where are we going?"

"You'll see," was all he would reply, but her question was soon answered when they stopped at a boating shop near the river. Nate explained that he'd managed to squeeze in a last-minute reservation for a rafting trip down the Adige River, which would afford them a different view altogether of Verona.

"When did you find time to call them?" Sarah exclaimed, and he grinned, clearly proud of himself. "I did it while you were in the shower Saturday morning. I wanted it to be a total surprise."

"Well, I am totally surprised," she said, joining the other tourists lining up for instructions on water safety and how to paddle their rafts. Soon the small company of guides and tourists was setting off down the gentle river for an alternative look at Verona.

Sarah had thought she couldn't see the city any differently, but she'd been wrong. Floating gently on the water, she wondered if trade vessels had once had this same view of a more ancient Verona.

She could see spires and church towers in the distance; the church bells were pealing softly. The red-tiled roofs rose on the gentle hills of the city, interspersed with trees; the morning sun reflected brightly off some of the whitewashed walls and illuminated the colourful paint or ageing brick of other buildings. She could almost imagine sailing into this city from a distant country, laden down with items for trade before embarking on another exotic voyage. She supposed medieval sea journeys were not as romantic as they seemed in her head, but it was fun to imagine all the same.

On the shore she could see people starting to emerge from homes and businesses, shaking off sleep and revelling in the sunshine. Their guide pointed out several famous sights as they drifted along, including the Castelvecchio that they'd visited earlier and the Torre dei Lamberti, a bell tower erected in the twelfth century.

The trip lasted a little over two hours, and by the end of it, Sarah was ready to eat again. The couple stopped for a quick snack at a street vendor before moving on to the Lamberti. The view from the top encompassed all of Verona; outside of the city gentle country hills were covered with trees, and in the far distance they could see mountains.

While there, they were taken aback when a strange man with a camera approached them to say that he'd taken a photograph of them a day or two earlier.

Sarah was sure that it was some tourist scam, but then the man introduced himself in an Irish accent and explained that he'd seen them together at the Piazza Bra and couldn't help snapping their picture.

They'd reminded him of something he explained, looking almost sheepish. "I hope you don't mind? If you give me an e-mail address I can send it to you."

Though still a little caught off-guard at the notion, Sarah could tell that the man was genuine and there was a sadness in his eyes that made her warm to him. She assured him that they didn't mind in the least, and found a scrap of paper in her bag on which she jotted down her e-mail.

"Are you visiting Verona alone, or with friends?" Nate asked him casually.

For a moment the man's face shuttered. "Alone," he said, trying to smile, explaining that his wife had died and he was visiting all the landmarks she would have wanted to see.

Sarah felt a fresh pang for him. To lose a spouse would be hard enough, and she could only imagine how it must feel to visit a place like this without the love of your life.

As they parted ways, she felt a fresh wave of appreciation for Nate. Despite their problems, weren't they blessed to both be still around to work them out?

He seemed to be thinking the same thing as she felt him squeeze her hand as they looked out from the tower.

Below the city streets were now full of people moving about with their Sunday business—families going out to eat lunch, tourists snapping pictures, and locals with a day off strolling through the streets and enjoying the mild weather. For the moment Nate and Sarah were alone at the top of the tower, and they lingered to enjoy the quiet.

Standing so high above the city, Sarah had the unreal feeling of floating above everything else. She moved closer to Nate and wrapped her arms around him. "Thank you for planning all of this out. It's wonderful."

"There's more yet to come," he said, smiling enigmatically.

Nate had found a place to rent vespas, and soon they were motoring around the city, climbing hills to stop in shady groves of trees, buying snacks and treats from street vendors, and stumbling upon statues and other small attractions that warranted a photo and a glance through the guidebook. They popped into a super-casual *osteria* for a late afternoon lunch; the short menu included a local speciality, donkey meat, which Nate gamely tried.

"Tastes like chicken," he whispered to Sarah with an exaggerated wink, and she smothered a laugh with her hand. She declined to try it, opting instead for actual chicken and a cold salad on the side. They returned to the Vespas and continued motoring through the city until evening fell, not really following a map or any guidebook, just going wherever their whims took them.

When evening came they dressed for dinner but despite the plethora of establishments in the city, they couldn't resist returning to Café Flores.

After the meal, as they stood waiting outside for a taxi back to their hotel, Sarah elbowed Nate in the ribs. "Look over there," she said in obvious awe. "That's Lily Forbes waiting for a taxi!"

Nate nudged her back. "Well, don't be shy. Go say hello."

Sarah did, and when she returned to Nate and climbed into the cab he said, "Well?"

"She said something surprising," Sarah said thoughtfully, but when he pressed her for more info she only demurred with a smile.

There was one more surprise waiting when they got back to their hotel: a call from the airline, saying that their luggage would be arriving on Tuesday.

"Tuesday?" Sarah exclaimed in dismay. "But we'll be back in the States by then."

"I guess we'll have to call them and ask

them to reroute it," Nate said, one hand on the phone. Then he paused.

The couple looked at each other for a long moment before both breaking into grins. Nate set the phone back on the table. "Or maybe we could just stick around a little longer."

CHAPTER 23

Lily flew back to London in a whirlwind of jotted-down notes and plans for her book.

In a fit of newfound pique, she stashed her heels in her suitcase and wore her flats through the airport.

Sod it, they were comfortable. However she still made sure to touch up her mascara before the plane landed.

She was standing alongside the baggage carousel at Heathrow waiting for her stuff when she heard a familiar voice. "Lily, is that you? It's been months."

She turned with some irritation to see Nick, her city trader ex. He was looking dapper as usual: tanned, well-dressed as always, with a smile on his face. He looked as though he'd been hitting the gym since she'd last seen him.

She had to admit he looked good though.

Her bags came down the belt, and before she could grab them he lifted them easily off the belt and placed them at her feet. "Flying out?"

"Flying in, actually," she replied. "From Verona." She could see by the look on his face that he was surprised to hear it, and was curious to know what she was doing there. Also, she thought, he was probably curious to know whom she'd travelled with. She wasn't going to give him the satisfaction of volunteering information, so she just smiled sweetly at him. "And what are you doing here?"

"On the way back from a business trip," he said, but he had a bit of a guilty look that made her guess there was pleasure involved, too. Not that she cared anymore, she reminded herself, and she grabbed her bags and said in a tone more chipper than she felt, "Well, it was wonderful to run into you. Enjoy your flight."

She didn't look back as she walked away, but she was certain he was staring after her in dismay. Nick wasn't used to being ignored, especially not by women.

Sure enough, as she walked outside she heard him calling her name. "Lily, wait!"

She paused, and he came running after her. "Babe, I've been meaning to call you for so long. It was a terrible mistake to break up with you. I miss you. Why don't we give it another go - you and me?"

She gave him a long look that he took for hesitation, and he touched her arm, adding in a seductive tone of voice, "I could cancel this trip. We could jet away somewhere, just the two of us. Somewhere romantic? Like Paris or something."

Lily looked at him for a long moment, her breath caught in her throat. Yes, they'd had some romantic times. Nick did indeed pull out all the stops with weekends away, gifts and grand gestures like the time he had four dozen roses sent to her apartment for no reason other than to say "I love you". And after so many months of being single, the sight of him was certainly tempting. He was an attractive man and knew it, and she thought of some of their more passionate times together with a hint of heat in her cheeks.

Then she chuckled, confusing him. "Nick, what we had was great for...about three months. But it's best left in the past. I've moved on; you should too."

He stared at her in absolute bewilderment; she could almost see the hamster wheel turning in his mind, trying to understand what had just happened to him. "You've changed," he finally sputtered out. "What happened to you in Italy?"

A taxi pulled up outside the terminal, and Lily took her time loading her bags before answering. Turning to him with the most sugary smile she could manage, she said cryptically, "I found Juliet."

Nick was still staring in confusion as she climbed into the cab and sped away.

While the driver wove expertly through the dense traffic into Central London, Lily pulled out her mobile phone and scrolled through the phone book. When she came to Nick's number she pressed "delete" without a second thought. Smiling, she slipped the phone back into her bag and gazed out the window at the city around her.

So many people, all with stories to tell, and infinite possibilities once she started thinking outside the formulaic box she'd confined herself to for so long.

Yes, her writer's block was definitely gone now.

Lily liked to think she'd left it sitting in an empty courtyard in Verona.

CHAPTER 24

SARAH CROSSED AND RECROSSED HER LEGS AS she sat in O'Hare terminal, waiting for Nate to arrive with their luggage.

After the long weekend turned week-long stay in Verona, she'd been so full of good food, good wine and good conversation that she'd slept through most of the train ride from Verona to Rome. Nate had to wake her when they arrived at the station so they could catch a taxi to the airport. She'd tried to read on the flight home to Chicago but ended up dozing some more.

She shifted her attention to Lily Forbes' book in her hands, still amazed that she'd actually met the author in person, and in Verona of all places. She still hadn't made it more than a few chapters in, but it wasn't for lack of interest; she was just too full of happy memories of their long week to concentrate on the story.

Her mother had called on Monday to make sure she would be home Tuesday night for dinner; it was the monthly Fieldings family gathering and her parents naturally assumed she would be there.

When she said regretfully that she would still be in Verona, her mother sounded flabbergasted. "But I thought you were only staying for a long weekend? Why are you still there? Don't tell me you had trouble with the flights; Nate messed up your booking, didn't he?"

Sarah felt a surge of ire at this remark. "We're here because we decided that we wanted to stay a little longer, that's all." Unable to bite her tongue she added, "I wish you wouldn't run Nate down for no reason. You constantly look for reasons to find fault with him."

"I just think he doesn't do enough for you," her mother began mildly, but Sarah cut her off.

"He does more than enough for me, Mother. He loves me and I love him, and you have to get used to it. Or if you aren't going to accept him, then you'll have to accept not having me around as much, because I won't just leave him at home like a bad puppy because you dislike him."

Once she got off the phone Sarah felt equal parts elated and guilty. She'd never stood up to her parents quite like that before, and she was certain giving her mother an ultimatum would have negative consequences down the road, but it was worth the risk. Speaking her mind had never felt so good.

After that, she and Nate dined again at Café Flores on Tuesday night. Marco and Valentina were delighted to see them again and pleased that they'd extended their stay.

A loudspeaker announced flights leaving O'Hare and remarked on delays. Nate finally appeared in the lounge, but he was empty-handed.

Running his hand through his hair, he said in exasperation, "I don't know if we're the unluckiest travellers in the world this month, but they've lost the damned suitcases again! They said they'll be arriving at our house sometime next week."

Something about the situation struck Sarah as too funny to endure, and she started laughing. Nate stared at her for a moment before he joined in, and soon they were both doubled over.

"We could have gotten by with only our carry-ons," Sarah said, holding her stomach. "And to think, I was so worried about colour-coordinating all those outfits."

This brought on a fresh wave of laughter. Finally, Sarah stood. "I don't know about you, but I'm ready to go home." She laid her book down on the lounge seat.

Nate glanced at it. "Lily Forbes? I thought you loved her books, and even more so after meeting her. Aren't you taking it home?"

Sarah glanced back at the book with a little smile. "I did...but no. I'll let someone else enjoy it. I think I'd rather focus on writing my own romance with you than reading about someone else's. "

She already knew that Lily wouldn't mind.

And with that, Sarah and Nate joined hands and walked out of the airport.

EPILOGUE

CAFÉ FLORES ENJOYED A STEADY FLOW OF customers all year long and the month of December was no different.

As Marco and Valentina closed up their trattoria on New Year's Eve, they sent their customers into the night with wishes for good health for the year ahead and a promise to see them soon, as many of their customers were locals who made a habit of eating there on a regular basis.

After they had cleaned up their restaurant and retired to the apartment upstairs for the night, they sat down in their living room as they did every New Year's Eve and went through Café Flores's bulging guest book, as well as various letters and notes they'd received from happy customers throughout the year.

It was a long-held tradition and one Marco and Valentina honoured year after year.

There were two unopened letters and one recently-arrived package also still intact that stood out as having all come from abroad, and Valentina brought fresh coffee into the room to drink while they carried out their ritual.

One of the letters was postmarked from the US.

Dear Marco and Valentina,

You probably don't remember us, but we passed through your trattoria in June, while we were in Verona for our honeymoon. (Well, belated honeymoon, but that's beside the point) While we were there you gave us both some excellent advice on love and life in general, and we've taken it to heart. We've worked on making our marriage stronger instead of trusting fate to guide us. Thank you for the excellent food and excellent wisdom. When we return to Verona we will be sure to come back and visit you.

Love, Nate and Sarah

P.S. We got an early Christmas present this

year...we just found out we're expecting our first child! If it's a girl we will probably name her Juliet.

VALENTINA SMILED as she put the letter aside.

"Isn't it interesting?" she said to her husband. "So many people leave all of love to fate, instead of reaching out and taking control."

Marco picked up another piece of unopened mail and read it. This one was postmarked from Dublin and was in a large stiff envelope.

MARCO AND VALENTINA,

When I visited your trattoria I was still grieving the loss of my wife. I didn't know how to get over her death and my trip to your city was only because of a promise I made her. You told me that moving forward in life didn't have to mean moving on from her memory and that I shouldn't be afraid to be happy and whole again. It's something similar to a letter Hannah wrote to me before she died. Anyway, I just wanted to thank you for your kindness. I'm still struggling, but things are getting easier. I'd like to think eventu-

ally it won't hurt quite so bad but I guess time will tell.

Also, have included a photo of your beautiful restaurant.

Cheers.

Declan O'Neill.

Marco pulled out the photograph, an enlarged black and white print, from between two stiff pieces of cardstock.

It was a lovely, artsy shot of the interior of the trattoria; Marco and Valentina were in one corner of the shot, sitting at a table, smiling at each other and holding hands.

"Oh, how lovely!" said Valentina. "We'll have to frame it for the wall."

The next item was a mystery; it was a slightly heavy, medium-sized package with a London return address. Inside was a loosely bound manuscript with a note on top.

Dear Marco and Valentina,

I can't thank you enough for what you said to me when I visited you. You told me to stop looking for

Juliet and I would find her. Well, I tried to take your advice, and I think it worked. I've stopped trying to force love to fit where it shouldn't, and I'm not chasing that idea of a picture-perfect romance anymore. I feel more optimistic about love than I have in years.

Love doesn't have to make sense to make sense.

And best of all, I hit upon the perfect idea for my next book!

Letters of Love *won't be published until next year, but I wanted to send you an advance reading copy. I hope you enjoy it.*

Much Love,
Lily Forbes

VALENTINA LIFTED THE BOOK PROOF. The plot centred around a romance novelist who is so unlucky in love she's given up on it entirely. She's trying to write a modern-day version of "Romeo and Juliet" but has writer's block, so she goes to Verona for a dose of inspiration.

Now that she's sworn off the idea of love, it seems that fate has plans for her, and she finds romance in the city after reading a letter posted on Juliet's wall.

"Hmm," Valentina laughed, "I remember

this one. It sounds like she found inspiration from Juliet after all ..."

The couple sat quietly for a while, in that sort of contented silence that's never awkward with the ones you know and love so well.

Outside, a snow-covered Verona was settling into herself for the night, a few winter tourists snuggling into their beds in warm hotels, and locals shutting up their homes and dreaming of New Year's resolutions.

The Italian couple thought back over all the people who had come through the doors of Café Flores over the years, each with different ideas on love and life.

So many people, all searching for the magic of the city to change their lives.

But the couple now putting their coffee cups in the kitchen and retiring quietly for the night knew the real secret; the magic didn't lie in legends about people who had once lived in Verona.

It was in the hearts of people who decided to love and be loved and would let nothing— family, past heartbreak, or any other obstacle— stand in their way.

Printed in Great Britain
by Amazon

40935786R00088